RISE AGAIN

A TEEN'S GUIDE TO OVERCOMING LIFE'S CHALLENGES

Vernon J. DeFlanders

© Copyright Notice

Title of the Work:
Rise Again: A Teen's Guide to Overcoming Life's Challenges

Copyright Owner

Rights Reserved

ISBN:
979-8303776548

Publisher Information
Published by *Vernon J. DeFlanders*
https://sites.google.com/view/navigatinglifeslessons/home

Contact Information:
For permissions, licensing, or other inquiries, please contact:
Vernon J DeFlanders
DeflandersCo@gmail.com
Navigating Life's Lessons

Disclaimer: *Rise Again: A Teen's Guide to Overcoming Life's Challenges*

The views and opinions expressed in this book are those of the author and are based on research, personal experiences, and insights. This book is intended for informational and educational purposes only and does not constitute professional advice. Readers are encouraged to seek professional guidance for specific concerns or circumstances.

While every effort has been made to ensure accuracy, the author and publisher assume no responsibility for errors or omissions or for any consequences arising from the use of this book. Any references to organizations, individuals, or events are for illustrative purposes and do not imply endorsement or affiliation.

This work is not intended to offend or marginalize any individual or group. Its purpose is to encourage reflection, foster understanding, and promote positive change. Readers are encouraged to approach the content with an open mind and adapt the lessons to their unique situations.

Table Of Content

Chapter 1

UNDERSTANDING CHALLENGES

The Nature of Challenges

Challenges are an inevitable part of life, especially during the teenage years. They can come in various forms, from academic pressures and social dynamics to personal struggles and family issues. Understanding the nature of these challenges is crucial for young adults, as it helps them recognize that facing difficulties is a shared experience. By acknowledging that challenges are a normal part of growth, teens can begin to shift their perspective, viewing obstacles not just as roadblocks but as opportunities for personal development.

One of the defining characteristics of challenges is their unpredictability. Unlike planned events, challenges often arise unexpectedly, catching individuals off guard. This unpredictability can lead to feelings of anxiety and helplessness. However, it is essential to remember that everyone experiences challenges at some point. Learning to anticipate difficulties and preparing mentally can help teens cultivate resilience. Embracing the unknown can also foster adaptability, equipping young adults with the skills necessary to navigate future hurdles.

Another important aspect of challenges is their complexity. Not all challenges are straightforward; some may have multiple layers that require thoughtful consideration and problem-solving. For example, a teen struggling with academic performance may face issues related to time management, study habits, or even emotional well-being. By breaking down complex challenges into manageable parts, young adults can approach them systematically. This method not only eases the burden but also empowers teens to take control of their situations, leading to a sense of accomplishment when they make progress.

Moreover, challenges serve as catalysts for growth. They often push individuals out of their comfort zones, forcing them to develop new skills and perspectives. When faced with adversity, teens may discover strengths they never knew they had. This process of self-discovery is vital for personal development, as it builds confidence and resilience. Embracing challenges can transform a daunting experience into a powerful lesson, equipping young adults with tools that will be beneficial throughout their lives.

Finally, the nature of challenges is deeply interconnected with a support system. Friends, family, teachers, and mentors play a significant role in helping teens navigate tough times. Building strong relationships can provide the encouragement and guidance necessary to overcome obstacles. Sharing experiences with peers can also create a sense of solidarity, reminding young adults that they are not alone in their struggles. By fostering a supportive environment, teens can learn to face challenges with courage and determination, ultimately emerging stronger and more resilient.

Common Challenges Faced by Teens

Teens today face a myriad of challenges that can feel overwhelming and isolating. One of the most common difficulties is the pressure to fit in and be accepted by peers. Adolescence is a critical time for social development, and many young adults grapple with issues related to friendship dynamics, popularity, and self-esteem. This pressure can lead to anxiety and feelings of inadequacy, especially if a teen feels they do not measure up to their peers. The constant comparison, whether through social media or in-person interactions, can exacerbate these feelings and create a sense of loneliness.

Academic pressure is another significant challenge for many teenagers. With rising expectations from schools, parents, and society, teens often feel that their worth is tied to their grades and achievements. The competition for college admissions and scholarships can be intense, leading to stress and burnout. Balancing homework, extracurricular activities, and part-time jobs can leave little time for relaxation and self-care. This relentless pursuit of academic excellence can take a toll on mental health, leading to anxiety, depression, and a sense of being overwhelmed.

Family dynamics can also present challenges during the teenage years. As adolescents seek independence, they may experience conflicts with parents or guardians who have different expectations. Issues such as divorce, financial problems, or a lack of communication can create tension at home. Teens may feel caught between wanting to assert their independence and needing parental support. Navigating these complex relationships can be difficult, and many young adults struggle to find a balance that allows them to feel both supported and autonomous.

Mental health concerns are increasingly prevalent among teenagers, with many facing anxiety, depression, and other emotional struggles. The stigma surrounding mental health often prevents young adults from seeking help, leaving them feeling trapped in their challenges. Understanding that mental health is just as important as physical health is crucial for teens as they navigate their emotions and seek support. Developing coping strategies, such as mindfulness and self-care practices, can empower teens to manage their mental well-being effectively.

Lastly, the impact of technology and social media cannot be overlooked. While these platforms can foster connection, they can also contribute to feelings of inadequacy and isolation. Cyberbullying, unrealistic portrayals of life, and the pressure to maintain a certain online image can create additional stress for young adults. It's essential for teens to cultivate a healthy relationship with technology, recognizing when to disconnect and prioritize real-life interactions. By addressing these challenges head-on, teens can learn to navigate the complexities of their lives and emerge stronger and more resilient.

The Importance of Resilience

Resilience is the ability to bounce back from setbacks, adapt to change, and keep moving forward in the face of adversity. For young adults navigating the complexities of life, developing resilience is crucial. It equips you with the mental and emotional tools needed to handle challenges, whether they stem from academic pressures, social dynamics, or personal struggles. Understanding the importance of resilience can empower you to approach difficulties with a proactive mindset, seeing challenges not as insurmountable obstacles but as opportunities for growth.

One key aspect of resilience is the capacity to maintain a positive outlook, even when things seem bleak. This doesn't mean ignoring your feelings or pretending everything is fine; rather, it's about acknowledging the difficulties while also recognizing your strengths and potential for recovery. When you cultivate a positive mindset, you are more likely to find solutions and alternatives to your problems. This perspective shift can transform how you react to challenges, allowing you to see them as temporary situations rather than permanent failures.

Building resilience also involves developing effective coping strategies. Each setback you experience offers a chance to learn about yourself and how to manage stress. Whether it's through problem-solving techniques, engaging in creative outlets, or seeking support from friends and family, finding healthy ways to cope is essential. These strategies not only help you deal with current challenges but also prepare you for future ones. The more tools you have in your emotional toolbox, the better equipped you will be to handle life's ups and downs.

Moreover, resilience fosters a sense of independence and self-efficacy. As you learn to overcome obstacles, you gain confidence in your ability to face future challenges. This self-assurance can lead to taking on new responsibilities and pursuing opportunities that may have previously seemed daunting. When you believe in your capacity to recover and adapt, you are more likely to step outside of your comfort zone, leading to personal growth and new experiences.

Finally, resilience is not just a personal trait; it can be cultivated within communities and support systems. Surrounding yourself with positive influences—friends, mentors, or family members who encourage you to persevere—can significantly impact your ability to bounce back. Engaging with others who share similar experiences can provide valuable insights and support, reinforcing the idea that you are not alone in your struggles. By building connections and fostering a supportive environment, you create a foundation that enhances your resilience and prepares you to tackle whatever challenges life may throw your way.

Chapter 2

EMBRACING EMOTIONS

Recognizing Your Feelings

Recognizing your feelings is a crucial step in managing life's challenges. Often, young adults experience a whirlwind of emotions that can be overwhelming, making it difficult to pinpoint exactly what they are feeling. Emotions can range from joy and excitement to sadness and frustration, and understanding these feelings is essential for personal growth and resilience. By learning to identify your emotions, you can begin to understand their impact on your thoughts and behaviors, ultimately helping you respond to life's challenges more effectively.

One of the first steps in recognizing your feelings is to develop emotional awareness. This means paying attention to how you feel in different situations and acknowledging those feelings without judgment. It can be helpful to keep a journal where you write down your emotions throughout the day. For instance, you might note that you felt anxious before a big test or happy after spending time with friends. Over time, this practice can help you become more attuned to your emotional landscape, making it easier to recognize patterns and triggers.

Another important aspect of recognizing your feelings is understanding that emotions are valid. Many young adults experience societal pressure to suppress or ignore their feelings, especially negative ones. However, acknowledging that it is okay to feel sad, angry, or confused is vital for emotional health. Emotions serve as signals that something may need attention in your life. For example, feeling stressed might indicate that you need to reevaluate your schedule or seek support from friends or family. Embracing your feelings as part of the human experience can empower you to face challenges head-on.

In addition to awareness and validation, it is essential to learn how to express your feelings appropriately. Bottling up emotions can lead to bigger issues down the line, such as increased anxiety or depression. Finding healthy outlets for expression, such as talking to a trusted friend, creating art, or engaging in physical activity, can help you process what you are feeling. Effective communication is key; sharing how you feel with others can foster deeper connections and provide you with the support you need to bounce back from setbacks.

Finally, recognizing your feelings is not just about understanding the emotions you experience in the moment. It also involves reflecting on past experiences and how they made you feel. This reflection allows you to build resilience by learning from your emotional responses. Ask yourself what you felt during difficult times and how those feelings influenced your actions. By recognizing the lessons within your emotions, you can better prepare for future challenges and develop a stronger sense of self. Embracing this journey of emotional recognition will ultimately help you rise again, transforming setbacks into opportunities for growth.

Healthy Ways to Express Emotions

Healthy expression of emotions is crucial for young adults navigating the complex journey of adolescence. Emotions serve as valuable signals that provide insights into our experiences and reactions. However, knowing how to express these feelings constructively can sometimes be challenging. It is important to adopt healthy outlets to ensure that emotions do not build up and lead to negative consequences. By understanding and implementing effective ways to express emotions, you can enhance your emotional well-being and resilience.

One effective method for expressing emotions is through journaling. Writing about feelings allows for introspection and helps clarify thoughts. When you put pen to paper, you create a space to explore what you are experiencing without judgment. Journaling can serve as a safe outlet for anger, sadness, or frustration, enabling you to process these feelings rather than suppress them. Additionally, revisiting your entries over time can reveal patterns in your emotional responses, empowering you to recognize and manage them more effectively.

Another healthy way to express emotions is through art. Engaging in creative activities such as drawing, painting, or crafting can provide a therapeutic release for your feelings. Art allows individuals to visualize their emotions and communicate them in a non-verbal manner. Whether you are creating a piece that reflects joy, sadness, or confusion, the act of creating can be cathartic. Sharing your artwork with others can also foster connection and understanding, as it opens up pathways for conversations about feelings and experiences.

Physical activity is a powerful tool for emotional expression as well. Exercise releases endorphins, which are neurotransmitters that promote feelings of happiness and reduce stress. Engaging in activities like running, dancing, or team sports not only helps to alleviate negative emotions but also provides an opportunity to channel feelings into something productive. Finding a physical outlet can help you cope with overwhelming emotions and improve your overall mood. It can also serve as a healthy distraction, allowing you to step back from what you're feeling and regain perspective.

Lastly, talking to someone you trust can be one of the most impactful ways to express your emotions. Whether it's a friend, family member, or counselor, verbalizing your feelings can lighten the emotional load. Conversations create opportunities for support, validation, and understanding. Sometimes, simply sharing what you're going through can help to clarify your thoughts and feelings. It is essential to choose someone who listens without judgment and can offer constructive feedback. This connection can foster resilience and remind you that it's okay to seek help when needed.

In conclusion, finding healthy ways to express emotions is vital for emotional health and overall well-being. Journaling, engaging in art, participating in physical activity, and having open conversations are all effective strategies that can aid in managing feelings. By adopting these methods, you can build a solid foundation for resilience, enabling you to navigate the challenges of adolescence more effectively. Remember, it's important to embrace your emotions and express them in ways that promote healing and growth.

The Role of Empathy in Overcoming Struggles

Empathy is a powerful tool that can significantly influence how we face and overcome struggles in life. At its core, empathy is the ability to understand and share the feelings of others. When we practice empathy, we cultivate a deeper connection with those around us, which can be incredibly beneficial during challenging times. For young adults navigating the ups and downs of adolescence, empathy not only strengthens relationships but also fosters resilience. Understanding that others have faced similar struggles can help normalize feelings of discomfort and uncertainty.

One of the primary benefits of empathy is the sense of community it creates. When teens share their experiences and challenges, it helps to break down barriers and diminish feelings of isolation. Knowing that others understand what you're going through can be comforting and empowering. This shared experience can lead to discussions that provide insights and coping strategies, making it easier to find solutions to personal struggles. Empathy encourages open communication, allowing young adults to express their feelings without fear of judgment.

Moreover, empathy can enhance emotional intelligence, an essential skill for managing life's challenges. By learning to recognize and interpret the emotions of others, teens can better navigate their feelings and responses. This heightened awareness can lead to improved decision-making and conflict resolution skills. When young adults practice empathy, they learn to approach situations with an open mind and a compassionate heart, which can help them tackle challenges more effectively. Instead of reacting impulsively, they become more thoughtful and considerate, which can lead to more successful outcomes.

Empathy also plays a crucial role in self-reflection and personal growth. When young adults engage in empathetic practices, they often find themselves reflecting on their own experiences and emotions. This introspection can lead to greater self-awareness and understanding of their struggles. By acknowledging their feelings and recognizing how they relate to the experiences of others, teens can develop healthier coping mechanisms. This process of reflection not only aids in overcoming current challenges but also prepares them for future obstacles, equipping them with a toolkit of strategies to draw from.

In conclusion, empathy is an essential component in overcoming struggles for young adults. By fostering connections, enhancing emotional intelligence, and promoting self-reflection, empathy empowers teens to face life's challenges with resilience and courage. As they learn to understand and support others, they simultaneously build a strong support network for themselves. Embracing empathy not only enriches their lives but also creates a ripple effect, encouraging a culture of compassion and understanding among peers, ultimately leading to a more supportive and resilient community.

Chapter 3

BUILDING A SUPPORT SYSTEM

Identifying Your Support Network

Identifying your support network is a crucial step in overcoming challenges and bouncing back from setbacks. A support network consists of people who provide emotional, practical, and sometimes even financial assistance during difficult times. These individuals can include family members, friends, teachers, coaches, and mentors. Recognizing who is part of your support network can empower you to seek help when you need it, making it easier to navigate life's ups and downs.

The first step in identifying your support network is to take a moment to reflect on the people in your life. Start by listing family members who you feel comfortable talking to about your struggles. This could be parents, siblings, or extended family like aunts, uncles, or grandparents. These individuals often have a deep understanding of your background and can provide valuable insights and encouragement. Consider their availability and willingness to listen, as well as their ability to offer guidance when you face challenges.

Next, think about your friends and peers. Friends can play a significant role in your support network, especially when it comes to sharing experiences and feelings. They may be going through similar challenges and can empathize with your situation. Identify those friends who are reliable, trustworthy, and understanding. These friendships can be a source of strength, allowing you to express your feelings openly and know that you are not alone in your struggles.

In addition to family and friends, consider adults in your life who could serve as mentors or guides. This might include teachers, coaches, school counselors, or community leaders. These individuals often have more life experience and can offer valuable advice and perspective. They can also help connect you with additional resources, whether that be academic help, extracurricular activities, or even mental health support. Building relationships with these adults can provide you with a broader support network that can help you navigate various challenges.

Finally, remember that your support network is not static; it can evolve over time. As you grow and change, so will the people around you. Stay open to forming new connections and strengthening existing ones. Engaging in community activities, clubs, or sports can introduce you to new peers and mentors who can become part of your support system. By actively cultivating your network, you create a sense of belonging and resilience that can help you rise again, no matter what obstacles you face.

Communicating with Friends and Family

Communicating with friends and family is essential in navigating the challenges of adolescence. During tough times, having a solid support system can make all the difference. Open and honest communication allows you to express your feelings, seek advice, and feel understood. This connection can help alleviate feelings of isolation and stress. Understanding how to effectively communicate with those closest to you can empower you to handle life's challenges more effectively.

When talking to friends, it is important to choose the right moment and setting. Find a comfortable space where you can both feel relaxed and open. Be clear about what you want to discuss, whether it's sharing your feelings about a recent setback or seeking advice on how to cope with a difficult situation. Listening is equally important; it shows that you value their perspective and strengthens your bond. Active listening involves giving your full attention, asking follow-up questions, and reflecting on what they say, which makes conversations more meaningful.

Family communication can sometimes feel more complicated due to differing perspectives, but it is equally vital. Start by identifying a family member you feel comfortable with. Approach them at a time when they are not preoccupied. Use "I" statements to express how you feel, such as "I feel overwhelmed when I face challenges." This approach reduces the chance of sounding accusatory and fosters a more constructive dialogue. Be patient, as family dynamics can take time to adjust, but your willingness to communicate can pave the way for deeper understanding.

Non-verbal communication also plays a key role in how your messages are received. Body language, facial expressions, and tone of voice can all convey emotions just as strongly as words. Being aware of these factors can help you express yourself more clearly and understand how others are feeling. For example, if a friend seems withdrawn, they might need a gentle nudge to open up. Being attuned to these cues can enhance your interactions and strengthen your relationships.

Lastly, remember that it's okay to seek help from professionals if needed. Sometimes, friends and family might not have all the answers, and that's perfectly normal. Therapists and counselors can provide guidance and strategies to cope with challenges effectively. Encouraging open communication about seeking help can normalize this process and reduce any stigma associated with it. By fostering a culture of communication within your circle, you can create a supportive environment that not only helps you bounce back from setbacks but also encourages growth and resilience.

Seeking Help from Professionals

Seeking help from professionals can be a crucial step in navigating the challenges that teens often face. Many young adults experience a range of emotions and situations that can feel overwhelming, from academic pressures to personal relationships. When these challenges become too difficult to manage alone, reaching out for professional support can provide the guidance and tools necessary to cope more effectively. Professional help can come in various forms, including counselors, therapists, and even trusted teachers or coaches who can offer valuable advice.

Counselors and therapists are trained to help individuals explore their feelings and thoughts in a safe, confidential environment. They can assist in identifying specific issues that may be causing distress, such as anxiety, depression, or family conflicts. For many teens, talking to someone who is unbiased and has experience in dealing with similar issues can be incredibly liberating. It can also lead to developing coping strategies that empower young adults to handle their challenges independently in the future.

In addition to traditional therapy, there are numerous resources available for teens seeking help. Many schools offer counseling services where students can speak with a professional without the stigma that sometimes accompanies seeking help outside of school. Additionally, online platforms and hotlines provide immediate support and guidance for those who may not feel comfortable seeking face-to-face help. These resources can be particularly beneficial for teens who may feel isolated or unsure about how to take the first step in seeking assistance.

Engaging with professionals not only helps in addressing immediate concerns but also contributes to long-term personal growth. Professionals can provide insights into behavioral patterns and thought processes that may hinder a teen's ability to bounce back from setbacks. By understanding these patterns, young adults can learn to reframe their perspectives, develop resilience, and cultivate a more positive outlook on their lives. This growth is essential for overcoming obstacles and building a foundation for future success.

Ultimately, seeking help is a sign of strength, not weakness. It shows a willingness to confront challenges head-on and take proactive steps toward improving one's situation.

Young adults should remember that they do not have to face their struggles alone. By reaching out to professionals, they can gain the support and resources needed to rise again, turning their setbacks into comebacks. Embracing this process can lead to a more fulfilling and empowered life, equipping them with the skills to tackle whatever challenges lie ahead.

Chapter 4

DEVELOPING A POSITIVE MINDSET

The Power of Positive Thinking

The concept of positive thinking is more than just a catchy phrase; it represents a powerful mindset that can significantly influence how young adults navigate life's challenges. Positive thinking involves focusing on the bright side of situations, maintaining an optimistic outlook, and believing in one's ability to overcome obstacles. This mindset is crucial for teens, as it can lead to improved mental health, better decision-making, and increased resilience in the face of adversity. By cultivating positive thinking habits, you can empower yourself to face setbacks with confidence and determination.

Research has shown that a positive outlook can enhance overall well-being and improve one's ability to cope with stress. When young adults adopt a positive thinking approach, they are more likely to engage in problem-solving behaviors rather than succumbing to despair. This proactive attitude enables them to see challenges not as insurmountable barriers, but as opportunities for growth and learning. By reframing negative thoughts and focusing on potential solutions, teens can transform their perspectives and foster a greater sense of control over their lives.

One practical way to cultivate positive thinking is through the practice of gratitude. By regularly acknowledging the things you appreciate in your life, whether big or small, you can shift your focus away from negativity and cultivate a more optimistic mindset. Keeping a gratitude journal, where you write down three things you are thankful for each day, can serve as a powerful reminder of the positives in your life. This simple yet effective practice can enhance your mood, boost your self-esteem, and help you approach challenges with a renewed sense of hope and possibility.

In addition to gratitude, surrounding yourself with positive influences is essential. The people you spend time with can significantly affect your mindset. Engaging with friends, family, or mentors who encourage you and inspire you to think positively can reinforce your own optimistic outlook. On the contrary, distancing yourself from negative influences can help create a supportive environment conducive to personal growth. Remember that you have the power to choose your circle, and selecting those who uplift you can make a substantial difference in your journey toward resilience.

Lastly, practicing self-compassion is a vital component of positive thinking. It involves treating yourself with kindness and understanding, especially during difficult times. Instead of harshly criticizing yourself for perceived failures or shortcomings, practice speaking to yourself as you would to a close friend. Recognizing that everyone faces challenges and that setbacks are a natural part of life can help alleviate feelings of inadequacy. By embracing self-compassion, you can foster a more positive internal dialogue, build resilience, and empower yourself to rise again after setbacks, ultimately becoming stronger and more capable of overcoming future challenges.

Overcoming Negative Self-Talk

Negative self-talk can be a significant barrier to achieving personal goals and maintaining a positive self-image. For many young adults, the internal dialogue can be harsh and relentless, often amplifying feelings of inadequacy and self-doubt. This self-critical voice may stem from various sources, including social pressures, academic challenges, and unrealistic comparisons with peers. Acknowledging the impact of negative self-talk is the first step toward overcoming it and fostering a healthier mindset.

Recognizing negative self-talk is essential for change. Pay attention to the thoughts that surface during challenging moments, especially when facing setbacks or failures. These thoughts often manifest as harsh critiques, such as "I'll never be good enough" or "I always mess things up." By identifying these patterns, you can begin to differentiate between constructive criticism and harmful negativity. Journaling can be a useful tool for tracking these thoughts and reflecting on their origins, helping you to understand and challenge them more effectively.

Once you have identified negative self-talk, it's crucial to challenge these thoughts. Ask yourself whether these beliefs are based on facts or if they stem from fear or insecurity. Often, the things we tell ourselves are exaggerated or unfounded. Reframing these thoughts into something more constructive can be transformative. For example, instead of saying "I failed my test, so I'm a failure," you might reframe it to "I didn't do well this time, but I can learn from my mistakes and do better next time." This shift in perspective not only alleviates pressure but also cultivates resilience.

Another effective strategy for overcoming negative self-talk is to practice self-compassion. Treat yourself with the same kindness and understanding that you would extend to a friend in a similar situation. When faced with a setback, remind yourself that everyone experiences challenges and that it's a natural part of growth. Engaging in positive affirmations can also help reinforce a healthier self-image. By regularly telling yourself affirming statements, such as "I am capable" or "I am worthy of love and respect," you can gradually replace negative thoughts with a more positive narrative.

Finally, surrounding yourself with supportive individuals can significantly impact your ability to combat negative self-talk. Friends, family, and mentors who encourage you and provide constructive feedback can serve as a buffer against the harshness of self-criticism. Engage in open conversations about your feelings and experiences, as sharing can lighten the emotional load and foster a sense of community. Building a supportive network empowers you to rise above negativity and strengthens your resolve to face life's challenges with confidence and resilience.

Techniques for Cultivating Optimism

Cultivating optimism is essential for navigating the challenges of adolescence. One effective technique is practicing gratitude. By taking time each day to reflect on the positive aspects of life, young adults can shift their focus away from negativity. This can be done through journaling, where individuals write down three things they are grateful for each day. This simple practice helps to reinforce a positive mindset, making it easier to cope with setbacks and recognize the silver linings in difficult situations.

Another valuable technique is visualization. Young adults can create mental images of their goals and the positive outcomes they desire. This process involves imagining not only the end result but also the steps needed to achieve those goals. By vividly picturing success, individuals can boost their confidence and motivation, which are crucial for overcoming obstacles. Visualization can be particularly powerful when combined with positive affirmations, where teens repeat encouraging phrases to themselves, reinforcing their belief in their abilities.

Engaging in mindfulness and meditation is another effective way to cultivate optimism. These practices allow young adults to become more aware of their thoughts and feelings, helping them to develop a more balanced perspective. Mindfulness encourages teens to live in the moment, preventing them from dwelling on past mistakes or worrying excessively about the future. Regular meditation can also reduce stress and anxiety, making it easier for individuals to maintain a hopeful outlook even in challenging circumstances.

Building a supportive social network is crucial for fostering optimism. Surrounding oneself with positive, encouraging friends and mentors can significantly impact mindset and resilience. Young adults should seek out relationships that inspire them and provide constructive feedback. Participating in group activities, clubs, or sports can also create a sense of belonging and community, reinforcing the idea that they are not alone in facing life's challenges.

Finally, setting realistic goals and celebrating small achievements can greatly enhance optimism. Young adults should break larger goals into manageable steps, allowing them to experience a series of successes along the way. Celebrating these milestones, no matter how small, helps to build confidence and reinforces a positive self-image. By acknowledging progress, teens can maintain motivation and optimism, making it easier to tackle future challenges with resilience and hope.

Chapter 5

SETTING GOALS

The Importance of Goal Setting

Goal setting is a crucial skill for young adults as it provides direction and purpose in life. It acts as a roadmap, allowing you to visualize where you want to go and what you need to do to get there. By establishing clear and achievable goals, you can break down your aspirations into manageable steps. This approach not only makes large objectives feel less daunting but also helps track your progress over time. When you see how far you've come, it can boost your motivation and reinforce your commitment to achieving your dreams.

Setting goals also enhances your decision-making skills. When you have a clear idea of what you want to achieve, making choices becomes simpler. You can evaluate opportunities based on whether they align with your goals. For instance, if your goal is to improve your grades, you might decide to spend more time studying rather than hanging out with friends. This ability to prioritize and make informed decisions is a vital skill that will serve you well throughout your life, helping you navigate both academic and personal challenges.

Moreover, goal setting fosters personal accountability. By defining specific goals, you create a sense of responsibility for your actions. You learn to hold yourself accountable for your progress, which cultivates discipline and perseverance. When you encounter setbacks, as everyone does, goal setting reminds you of your ultimate objectives and encourages you to push through difficulties. This resilience is essential for overcoming obstacles and bouncing back from adversity, reinforcing the belief that you can achieve what you set out to do.

Another important aspect of goal setting is that it can significantly boost your self-confidence. Achieving even small goals can provide a sense of accomplishment and empower you to tackle bigger challenges. As you meet your goals, you begin to build a track record of success, which helps to reinforce your belief in your abilities. This newfound confidence can spill over into other areas of your life, making you more willing to take risks and pursue opportunities that once seemed out of reach.

Finally, goal setting encourages reflection and growth. Regularly reviewing your goals allows you to assess your progress and make necessary adjustments. This process of reflection fosters a growth mindset, where you view challenges as opportunities to learn rather than insurmountable barriers. Embracing this mindset can transform how you approach life's challenges, equipping you with the tools necessary to rise again after setbacks. By understanding the importance of setting and pursuing goals, you are taking a significant step towards realizing your potential and crafting a fulfilling future.

SMART Goals Explained

SMART goals are a powerful tool that can help you navigate the challenges of adolescence and set you on a path toward success. The acronym SMART stands for Specific,

Measurable, Achievable, Relevant, and Time-bound. Each component plays a crucial role in helping you develop clear and actionable goals, making it easier to focus your efforts and track your progress. By understanding and applying the SMART framework, you can effectively turn your aspirations into concrete achievements.

To start with, Specific goals are clear and well-defined. Instead of saying, "I want to get better at math," a specific goal would be, "I want to improve my math grade from a C to a B by the end of the semester." This clarity helps you understand exactly what you are aiming for, eliminating any ambiguity. When you know precisely what you want to achieve, it becomes easier to create a plan that targets that goal directly.

Next, Measurable goals allow you to track your progress. A measurable goal includes criteria to evaluate your advancement. For example, instead of saying, "I want to exercise more," a measurable goal would be, "I will exercise for at least 30 minutes three times a week." This way, you can monitor your efforts and see how far you've come, which can be motivating and help you stay committed to your goal.

Achievable goals are realistic and attainable, considering your current circumstances and resources. Setting an achievable goal means that you consider what is possible within your skill level and time constraints. For instance, rather than aiming to become the top athlete in your school in just one month, a more achievable goal could be, "I will practice my sport for an hour every Saturday." This approach fosters a sense of accomplishment, as you are more likely to succeed when your goals are within reach.

Relevant goals ensure that what you are working toward aligns with your interests and values. A relevant goal should matter to you and contribute to your overall growth. For instance, if you want to pursue a career in writing, a relevant goal might be, "I will complete a short story every month." This goal is meaningful and directly ties to your long-term aspirations. Lastly, Time-bound goals have a clear deadline, which creates a sense of urgency and helps you prioritize your efforts. For example, saying, "I will complete my project by next Friday" gives you a timeline to work within, pushing you to stay focused and organized. By incorporating these elements into your goal-setting process, you can create a roadmap that guides you through life's challenges and empowers you to rise again after setbacks.

Breaking Down Bigger Goals into Manageable Steps

Setting big goals can often feel overwhelming, especially for young adults navigating the complexities of life. When faced with significant ambitions, it can be challenging to determine where to start. However, breaking down larger goals into manageable steps can make the process more approachable and less intimidating. This strategy not only provides clarity but also enhances motivation as you celebrate small victories along the way.

The first step in breaking down your goals is to clarify what you want to achieve. Take some time to reflect on your larger goal and articulate it in specific terms. For instance, if your goal is to improve your grades, define what that means for you: Is it achieving a certain GPA, mastering specific subjects, or developing better study habits? Once you have a clear vision, you can begin to dissect it into smaller, actionable components.

Once you have defined your goal, the next step is to create a list of smaller tasks that can lead you to your larger objective. For example, if your goal is to get a scholarship for college, consider the steps involved: researching potential schools, preparing for standardized tests, writing personal statements, and gathering recommendation letters. By identifying these smaller tasks, you create a roadmap to follow, making the journey feel more structured and less overwhelming.

Setting deadlines for each smaller task can further enhance your progress. When you assign a timeline to each step, you create a sense of urgency that can propel you forward. For instance, if you aim to complete a personal statement by a certain date, you can break that down into tasks such as brainstorming ideas, drafting, revising, and seeking feedback. This approach helps you manage your time effectively and stay focused on your objectives without feeling lost in the bigger picture.

Lastly, it is crucial to celebrate your achievements along the way. Acknowledging the completion of each smaller task reinforces your motivation and reminds you of the progress you are making. Whether it's treating yourself to a favorite snack, spending time with friends, or simply taking a moment to reflect on how far you've come, these celebrations can help maintain your enthusiasm. Remember, every small step you take brings you closer to your larger goal, and each one is worth recognizing.

Chapter 6

LEARNING FROM SETBACKS

Analyzing What Went Wrong

Analyzing what went wrong is a crucial step in overcoming setbacks and challenges in life. When faced with difficulties, it's natural to feel overwhelmed or frustrated, but taking the time to dissect the situation can provide valuable insights. This process begins with honest self-reflection. Ask yourself what specific events led to the setback. Was it a decision you made? Did external factors play a role? Understanding the root cause is essential for preventing similar situations in the future.

Once you identify the root cause, consider your emotions during the experience. Emotions can cloud judgment and lead to decisions that may not align with your best interests. Reflecting on how you felt at the time can help you understand your reactions and choices. Were you feeling anxious, pressured, or fearful? Recognizing these emotions allows you to develop strategies for managing them in future situations, enabling you to approach challenges with a clearer mindset.

Next, it's important to evaluate the choices you made. Every setback is an opportunity to learn, and analyzing your decisions can reveal patterns in your behavior. Did you rush into a decision without considering the consequences? Did you seek advice from trusted friends or mentors? By examining these choices, you can pinpoint areas for improvement and build a toolkit of effective strategies for decision-making. This self-awareness will empower you to make better choices going forward.

Additionally, consider the role of external influences in your situation. Sometimes, setbacks are influenced by factors outside of your control, such as peer pressure, societal expectations, or unforeseen circumstances. Recognizing these influences does not mean you are absolved of responsibility; rather, it helps you understand the broader context of your experiences. This understanding can foster resilience, as you learn to navigate and adapt to the challenges presented by the world around you.

Finally, after dissecting the situation, it's crucial to create an actionable plan for the future. Use the insights gained from your analysis to develop specific goals and strategies. This might involve setting clear boundaries, seeking support from others, or practicing skills such as stress management and decision-making. By turning your reflections into a concrete plan, you take control of your journey and set yourself up for success. Remember, analyzing what went wrong is not about dwelling on mistakes but about learning and growing stronger for what lies ahead.

Finding the Silver Lining

Finding the silver lining in challenging situations can be a powerful tool for young adults navigating the tumultuous journey of adolescence. Life is filled with ups and downs, and while it may feel overwhelming at times, each setback can also present an opportunity for growth and resilience. Understanding how to identify and embrace these positive aspects can help you develop a more optimistic perspective, allowing you to bounce back when faced with obstacles.

One of the first steps in finding the silver lining is to practice gratitude. Taking a moment to reflect on what you appreciate in your life, even during tough times, can shift your mindset. Keeping a gratitude journal can be an effective way to document the small joys that occur each day. This practice helps you focus on the positives, making it easier to see the good amid the challenges. By recognizing what you are thankful for, you can create a mental buffer against negativity and develop a more hopeful outlook.

Another important aspect of finding the silver lining is to reframe negative experiences. Instead of viewing a setback as a failure, try to see it as a learning experience. Ask yourself what lessons can be taken from the situation and how they can inform your future decisions. For instance, if you didn't perform well on a test, consider what study strategies didn't work and how you can improve for next time. This change in perspective allows you to transform feelings of disappointment into motivation to do better, reinforcing your resilience in the face of adversity.

Connecting with others during difficult times can also help you uncover the silver lining. Sharing your experiences with friends, family, or mentors can provide comfort and perspective. Often, others have faced similar challenges and can offer insights that help you see the situation in a new light. Building a support system encourages collaboration and understanding, reminding you that you are not alone in your struggles. This sense of community can foster hope and empower you to find the positive side of your experiences.

Lastly, cultivating a mindset of optimism is essential in the journey of finding the silver lining. This involves actively choosing to focus on potential solutions rather than dwelling on problems. Engaging in positive self-talk and visualizing success can enhance your confidence and motivation. Remember that every challenge is temporary, and with perseverance, you can overcome obstacles. By embracing an optimistic outlook, you not only enhance your own well-being but also inspire those around you to do the same, creating a ripple effect of positivity in your community.

Turning Mistakes into Learning Opportunities

Mistakes are an inevitable part of life, especially during the teenage years when you are navigating new experiences and challenges. Rather than viewing mistakes as failures, it's essential to see them as opportunities for growth and learning. This shift in perspective can transform how you approach various situations, allowing you to bounce back stronger and more resilient. Each mistake provides valuable lessons if you're willing to reflect on them and apply what you've learned moving forward.

When you encounter a setback, take a moment to analyze what happened. Ask yourself questions like, "What went wrong?" and "What could I have done differently?" This self-reflection is key to understanding the root of the problem. It's not just about identifying the mistake, but also recognizing the factors that contributed to it. By breaking down the situation, you can gain insights into your decision-making processes and identify patterns that may need adjustment. This analytical approach helps you develop critical thinking skills that will serve you well in the future.

It's also important to remember that everyone makes mistakes. You are not alone in your experiences. Many successful individuals have faced significant setbacks before achieving their goals. Learning about their journeys can provide inspiration and reassurance that mistakes are merely stepping stones on the path to success. By sharing your own experiences with friends or mentors, you can foster a supportive environment where everyone learns from their missteps, creating a culture of resilience and growth.

Once you have reflected on your mistakes, it's time to take action. Use the lessons learned to make informed decisions in the future. This might involve setting new goals, changing your approach, or seeking guidance from others. Taking proactive steps not only helps you avoid repeating the same mistakes but also boosts your confidence. Each time you successfully navigate a challenge after a setback, you reinforce your ability to overcome obstacles, further solidifying your resilience.

Incorporating a mindset that embraces mistakes as learning opportunities can significantly enhance your personal growth. By acknowledging that mistakes are a natural part of life, you can reduce the fear of failure and open yourself up to new experiences. This positive outlook encourages exploration and creativity, allowing you to take calculated risks without the paralyzing fear of making mistakes. Ultimately, transforming mistakes into learning opportunities empowers you to rise again and face life's challenges with renewed strength and determination.

Chapter 7

BUILDING COPING STRATEGIES

Healthy Coping Mechanisms

Healthy coping mechanisms are essential tools for navigating the ups and downs of adolescence. During this time of significant change, young adults may face various stressors, including academic pressure, social dynamics, and personal challenges. Understanding and implementing healthy coping strategies can help manage stress effectively and promote emotional well-being. Recognizing the difference between healthy and unhealthy coping mechanisms is the first step toward developing a more resilient mindset.

One effective coping mechanism is engaging in physical activity. Exercise has been shown to reduce stress and anxiety while boosting mood through the release of endorphins. Whether it's participating in team sports, going for a run, or practicing yoga, finding a physical activity that you enjoy can provide an outlet for negative emotions and a way to clear your mind. Regular physical activity not only enhances physical health but also fosters a sense of achievement and self-esteem, which are crucial during adolescence.

Another healthy coping strategy involves practicing mindfulness and relaxation techniques. Mindfulness encourages individuals to remain present and fully engaged in the moment, which can significantly reduce feelings of anxiety and overwhelm. Techniques such as deep breathing, meditation, or progressive muscle relaxation can help calm the mind and body. Incorporating these practices into your daily routine can create a sense of balance and help you respond to challenges with a clearer perspective.

Building a strong support network is also vital for healthy coping. Surrounding yourself with friends, family, or mentors who understand and support your feelings can provide a sense of belonging and validation. Sharing your experiences and emotions with others can lighten the burden of stress and help you gain different perspectives on your challenges. Whether it's through casual conversations or more structured support groups, connecting with others can foster resilience and encourage you to seek help when needed.

Lastly, creative outlets can serve as powerful coping mechanisms. Engaging in artistic activities such as drawing, writing, music, or dance allows for self-expression and can be therapeutic. These creative pursuits provide an opportunity to process emotions and experiences in a constructive way. Exploring your creativity not only serves as a distraction from stress but also helps in developing new skills and discovering passions that can enhance your identity during these formative years. By incorporating these healthy coping mechanisms into your life, you can build resilience and effectively navigate the challenges of adolescence.

Mindfulness and Meditation

Mindfulness and meditation are powerful tools that can help young adults navigate the challenges of adolescence. In a world filled with constant distractions, social pressures, and emotional turmoil, these practices offer a way to find calm, clarity, and resilience. By cultivating mindfulness, you learn to focus on the present moment rather than getting lost in worries about the past or future. This shift in perspective can significantly reduce anxiety and improve your overall well-being.

Meditation, a key component of mindfulness, involves training your mind to achieve a state of focused attention and relaxation. While it might seem daunting at first, meditation can be practiced in various ways, making it accessible for everyone. Simple techniques, such as deep breathing or guided imagery, can help you develop the habit of meditating regularly. Even just a few minutes a day can lead to noticeable improvements in your mood, concentration, and stress levels.

One of the primary benefits of mindfulness and meditation is their ability to enhance emotional regulation. As a teenager, you may encounter a wide range of emotions, from joy to frustration, often feeling overwhelmed by them. Mindfulness encourages you to observe your feelings without judgment, allowing you to respond thoughtfully rather than react impulsively. This practice fosters greater emotional intelligence, helping you understand and manage your emotions more effectively.

In addition to emotional regulation, mindfulness can improve your relationships with others. When you practice being present, you become more attuned to the feelings and needs of those around you. This heightened awareness can lead to more meaningful conversations and connections with friends, family, and peers. By cultivating empathy and compassion through mindfulness, you can create a supportive network that helps you bounce back from setbacks.

Incorporating mindfulness and meditation into your daily routine can be transformative. Start with short sessions, gradually increasing the time as you become more comfortable with the practice. Consider using apps or online resources that offer guided meditations tailored for teens. Remember, the goal is not to achieve perfection but to develop a habit that supports your mental and emotional health. By embracing mindfulness and meditation, you equip yourself with valuable skills to face life's challenges head-on, ultimately enabling you to rise again stronger and more resilient.

Physical Activity as a Stress Reliever

Physical activity serves as a powerful tool for managing stress, especially for young adults navigating the complexities of adolescence. When faced with challenges such as academic pressure, social dynamics, and personal issues, many teens experience heightened levels of stress and anxiety. Engaging in regular physical activity can provide a healthy outlet for these emotions, offering both immediate and long-term benefits. Whether it's a brisk walk, a dance class, or a team sport, moving your body helps release tension and improve your overall mood.

One of the primary ways physical activity alleviates stress is through the release of endorphins, often referred to as "feel-good" hormones. These chemicals are released during exercise and can create a sense of euphoria, commonly known as the "runner's high." This natural high can lead to improved mood and a decrease in feelings of sadness or anxiety. Regular exercise not only helps combat stress but also builds resilience, allowing you to face challenges with a more positive mindset.

In addition to the hormonal benefits, physical activity encourages mindfulness and focus. When you engage in physical exercises, you often find yourself immersed in the moment, whether you're concentrating on your movements, enjoying the scenery during a jog, or working with teammates during a game. This focus helps divert your attention from stressors and negative thoughts, providing a mental break. Activities such as yoga or martial arts can offer additional mindfulness benefits, teaching you techniques to manage your thoughts and emotions effectively.

Social connections formed through physical activity can also play a significant role in reducing stress. Joining a sports team, attending a fitness class, or simply working out with friends fosters a sense of community and belonging. These social interactions can provide emotional support, as sharing experiences and challenges with peers can create a network of understanding and encouragement. Engaging in physical activities together can also lead to laughter and fun, further alleviating stress and strengthening friendships.

Lastly, incorporating physical activity into your routine can improve your overall well-being, which in turn helps reduce stress levels. Regular exercise enhances sleep quality, boosts energy levels, and improves concentration, all of which are vital for managing stress effectively. By prioritizing physical activity, you are not just improving your physical health but also equipping yourself with the tools needed to navigate life's challenges. Embracing movement as a form of stress relief can empower you to rise again, turning setbacks into comebacks with renewed strength and resilience.

Chapter 8

CULTIVAING GRIT AND PERSEVERANCE

Understanding Grit

Grit is a powerful quality that can significantly influence your ability to overcome challenges and achieve your goals. At its core, grit is a combination of passion and perseverance. It involves having the determination to pursue long-term goals, even in the face of obstacles and failures. While talent and intelligence are often celebrated, it is grit that can truly make the difference between success and giving up. Understanding grit can empower you to cultivate this essential trait in your own life.

One of the key components of grit is passion. This means having a deep interest in what you are pursuing. Whether it's a sport, a subject in school, or a creative endeavor, having passion fuels your motivation to keep going. Passion provides a sense of purpose and direction. When you are passionate about something, you are more likely to invest the time and energy required to improve and overcome setbacks. Identifying what you are truly passionate about can help you stay focused and committed, even when the going gets tough.

Perseverance is another crucial element of grit. It refers to the ability to keep pushing forward, even when faced with difficulties. Life is filled with challenges, and it's normal to encounter failure along the way. However, those with grit view failures as opportunities for growth rather than reasons to give up. They learn from their mistakes and use those lessons to become stronger. Developing a resilient mindset allows you to bounce back from disappointments and continue striving toward your aspirations.

Building grit is not something that happens overnight. It requires consistent effort and practice. One effective way to cultivate grit is by setting small, achievable goals that contribute to your larger objectives. Each time you achieve a goal, no matter how minor, you reinforce your ability to persevere and succeed. Additionally, surrounding yourself with supportive friends, mentors, and role models can help motivate you to stick to your commitments and push through tough times. Remember that grit is like a muscle; the more you use it, the stronger it becomes.

Ultimately, understanding and developing grit can lead to significant personal growth. It teaches you the value of hard work, resilience, and dedication. As you navigate through the challenges of adolescence, developing grit can help you face obstacles with confidence and determination. Embracing this quality not only prepares you to overcome setbacks but also sets you on a path toward achieving your dreams. By recognizing the importance of grit, you can learn to rise again, no matter how many times life tries to knock you down.

Real-Life Examples of Perseverance

Perseverance is a powerful trait that has been exemplified by many individuals throughout history. One notable example is Thomas Edison, the famous inventor known for creating the electric light bulb. Edison's journey was fraught with failures; he famously conducted thousands of experiments before finally achieving success. Each setback taught him something new, and instead of giving up, he viewed these challenges as stepping stones to his ultimate goal. His story illustrates that perseverance can lead to groundbreaking achievements and that failure is often just a part of the learning process.

Another inspiring example comes from Malala Yousafzai, a young activist for girls' education. Despite facing life-threatening opposition in her home country of Pakistan, Malala refused to be silenced. After surviving an assassination attempt, she continued to advocate for education rights on a global level. Her courage and determination in the face of adversity not only transformed her life but also inspired millions around the world. Malala's story is a reminder that standing up for one's beliefs, even in the face of danger, can create significant change and motivate others to persevere in their own struggles.

Athletes also embody perseverance, as seen in the journey of Michael Jordan. He faced rejection early in his career when he was cut from his high school basketball team. Rather than letting this setback define him, he dedicated himself to improving his skills, practicing relentlessly, and ultimately earning a spot on the team. Jordan went on to become one of the greatest basketball players of all time, showcasing that perseverance in the face of rejection can lead to extraordinary success. His story teaches young adults that resilience can turn obstacles into opportunities.

In the realm of arts, J.K. Rowling's experience with the Harry Potter series serves as a testament to perseverance. Before her books became a global phenomenon, Rowling faced numerous rejections from publishers, struggling as a single mother living on welfare. Despite the challenges, she continued to write and believe in her story. Her persistence paid off when a small publisher finally agreed to publish the first book, and the series went on to inspire millions of readers. Rowling's journey emphasizes that unwavering belief in one's vision can lead to triumph, even when the odds seem stacked against you.

Lastly, consider the story of Bethany Hamilton, a professional surfer who lost her arm in a shark attack. Rather than allowing this life-altering event to end her surfing career, she demonstrated remarkable resilience and determination. Hamilton trained herself to adapt and eventually returned to competitive surfing, inspiring others with her incredible comeback. Her story highlights that perseverance is not just about enduring hardships but also about embracing change and finding new ways to achieve one's passions. Through these real-life examples, it is evident that perseverance can help young adults navigate challenges and emerge stronger on the other side.

Practices to Enhance Grit

To enhance grit, it is essential for young adults to cultivate a mindset focused on perseverance and resilience. One effective practice is setting specific, achievable goals. By breaking larger aspirations into smaller, manageable tasks, you create a clear path forward. This approach allows you to celebrate small victories along the way, which can significantly boost your motivation and confidence. Each completed task reinforces the belief that you can overcome challenges, fostering a sense of accomplishment that fuels further effort.

Another vital practice is embracing failure as a learning opportunity. When setbacks occur, it is crucial to reflect on what went wrong and how you can improve in the future. Instead of viewing failure as a definitive end, see it as a stepping stone toward growth. This perspective shift encourages resilience and helps you develop a more robust approach to difficulties. Acknowledging that everyone experiences setbacks can normalize the process and make it easier to bounce back.

Building a supportive network is also key to enhancing grit. Surround yourself with friends, family, and mentors who encourage you to keep pushing forward. These relationships provide not only emotional support but also practical guidance during tough times. Engaging with others who have faced their own challenges can inspire you and offer valuable insights. When you feel connected to a community, it becomes easier to stay motivated and committed to your goals.

Practicing mindfulness is another effective tool for developing grit. Mindfulness techniques, such as meditation or deep-breathing exercises, can help you manage stress and stay focused on the present moment. By reducing anxiety and improving your emotional regulation, mindfulness allows you to approach challenges with a clearer mind. This mental clarity enables better decision-making and enhances your ability to persist in the face of adversity.

Lastly, nurturing a passion for continuous learning can significantly enhance your grit. Cultivating curiosity about new subjects or skills encourages you to step out of your comfort zone and embrace challenges. When you actively seek out new experiences, you become more adaptable and resilient. This lifelong learning mindset not only prepares you for future obstacles but also instills a sense of joy in the journey of personal growth. By integrating these practices into your daily life, you can strengthen your grit and better navigate the challenges that come your way.

Chapter 9

CELEBRATING SMALL VICTORIES

The Importance of Acknowledging Progress

Acknowledging progress is a crucial part of personal growth, especially for young adults navigating the challenges of adolescence. It's easy to get caught up in the pursuit of future goals and forget to recognize how far you've come. Celebrating small victories not only boosts your motivation but also reinforces a positive mindset. Understanding that every step you take, no matter how small, contributes to your overall journey can help you stay focused and resilient in the face of setbacks.

One of the key reasons acknowledging progress is important is that it builds self-confidence. When you take the time to reflect on what you've achieved, you create a tangible record of your efforts and successes. This can help counter feelings of self-doubt that often arise during difficult times. For instance, if you're struggling with schoolwork, recalling the improvements you've made over the semester can remind you of your capabilities. This acknowledgment can provide the encouragement needed to keep pushing forward, even when challenges feel overwhelming.

Additionally, recognizing progress fosters a sense of gratitude. By appreciating where you are now compared to where you started, you cultivate a mindset that values your journey. This gratitude can shift your focus from what you lack to what you have, which is crucial for maintaining motivation. When you celebrate achievements, no matter how minor, you create a more positive outlook on your life and the challenges you face. This perspective can make it easier to tackle obstacles and feel more connected to your goals.

Furthermore, acknowledging progress helps create a habit of reflection. Taking time to assess your journey encourages you to think critically about your experiences, decisions, and the lessons learned along the way. This habit of reflection can lead to deeper insights about yourself and your aspirations. When you regularly evaluate your progress, you become more adept at identifying patterns in your behavior and thinking, allowing you to make more informed choices in the future.

Lastly, sharing your progress with others can strengthen your support network. When you talk about your achievements with friends, family, or mentors, you not only celebrate your journey but also inspire those around you. This communal acknowledgment can create an atmosphere of encouragement and motivation, where everyone feels empowered to recognize and support one another's growth. In conclusion, acknowledging progress is not just about celebrating success; it's about building resilience, fostering gratitude, developing reflection habits, and strengthening connections with others.

Creating a Victory Journal

Creating a Victory Journal is an empowering practice that can help young adults recognize their achievements and build resilience. This journal serves as a personal space where you can document your successes, no matter how small they may seem. It is essential to understand that victories are not limited to major milestones; they can be everyday accomplishments that contribute to your overall growth and confidence. By acknowledging these moments, you can foster a positive mindset that encourages you to keep pushing through challenges.

To start your Victory Journal, choose a notebook or digital platform that resonates with you. The medium you select should inspire you to write freely and expressively. As you begin, think about what constitutes a victory for you. This could include completing a challenging assignment, making a new friend, or overcoming a fear. Write down the date and describe the victory in detail. Reflect on how it made you feel and what steps you took to achieve it. This practice not only reinforces your successes but also helps you understand the effort you put into reaching them.

Consistency is key to reaping the benefits of your Victory Journal. Set a regular schedule for writing in it, whether it's daily, weekly, or whenever you feel it necessary. Establishing a routine can help you stay focused on your progress and keep your spirits high, especially during tough times. Make it a habit to review your entries periodically. This reflection can serve as a reminder of your strengths and growth, especially when you face new obstacles. Over time, you will notice patterns in your victories and the skills you've developed, which can boost your self-esteem.

In addition to documenting victories, consider including sections for gratitude and goal-setting. Expressing gratitude for the positive aspects of your life can elevate your mood and shift your focus away from negativity. Setting goals in your journal can provide direction and motivation, allowing you to track your aspirations and celebrate the steps you take toward achieving them. Together, these elements create a comprehensive tool for personal development, helping you become more resilient in the face of life's challenges.

Finally, remember that your Victory Journal is a personal and unique reflection of your journey. There are no right or wrong ways to express yourself, so let your creativity shine through. You can incorporate drawings, quotes, or even photos that resonate with your experiences. As you fill your journal with victories, gratitude, and goals, you will cultivate a sense of empowerment that encourages you to rise again, no matter what life throws your way. Embrace this opportunity to celebrate yourself and your journey towards becoming the best version of you.

Sharing Success with Others

Sharing success with others is an essential aspect of personal growth and resilience. When we experience triumphs, whether big or small, it can be tempting to keep them to ourselves, basking in the glory of individual achievement. However, sharing these moments not only magnifies our own joy but also inspires and uplifts those around us. By celebrating our successes together, we create a supportive community that recognizes the importance of collaboration and mutual encouragement.

One of the most powerful ways to share success is through storytelling. When you recount your journey, including the challenges you faced and how you overcame them, you provide valuable insights to others who may be struggling. Your experiences can serve as a beacon of hope, demonstrating that setbacks are a natural part of life and that resilience can lead to positive outcomes. Sharing your story can encourage your peers to embrace their own struggles and strive for their goals, knowing that they are not alone in their journey.

Moreover, sharing success can foster a sense of accountability. When you openly discuss your achievements and goals with others, you create a network of support that can help you stay motivated. Friends, family, and mentors can offer encouragement and guidance, pushing you to maintain your momentum. This kind of communal support not only boosts your confidence but also reinforces the idea that success is not solely an individual endeavor—it's often the result of teamwork and collaboration.

In addition to personal connections, sharing success can also extend to your community. Engaging in volunteer work or mentoring younger peers allows you to use your experiences to make a positive impact on others. By sharing your knowledge and skills, you not only help someone else overcome their challenges but also reinforce your own achievements. This cycle of giving and receiving can create a ripple effect, inspiring others to rise above their difficulties and aspire to their own successes.

Finally, celebrating the successes of others is just as important as sharing your own. Acknowledging the accomplishments of your peers fosters a culture of positivity and motivation. When you cheer for others, you strengthen your relationships and cultivate an environment where everyone feels valued. This mutual recognition helps to build resilience within the community, as each individual learns to appreciate the journeys of others while also feeling encouraged to pursue their own goals. By embracing the philosophy of sharing success, we can all rise together, turning our triumphs into collective victories.

Chapter 10

LOOKING TO THE FUTURE

Visualizing Success

Visualizing success is a powerful tool that can help you turn your dreams into reality. It involves creating a mental image of your goals and imagining yourself achieving them. This practice not only helps clarify what you want but also prepares your mind to work towards those objectives. By honing in on your aspirations, you can develop a clearer roadmap of the steps you need to take to get there. Visualizing success can be particularly beneficial during challenging times, as it allows you to maintain focus and motivation even when setbacks occur.

One effective way to visualize success is through guided imagery, where you close your eyes and picture yourself in a future scenario where you have achieved your goals. This could be picturing yourself acing an important exam, successfully performing in a talent show, or overcoming a personal challenge. As you create this mental image, engage all your senses. Imagine the sounds, smells, and feelings associated with your success. The more vivid and detailed your visualization, the more impact it will have on your mindset and confidence.

Another method to enhance your visualization practice is to create a vision board. A vision board is a collage of images, quotes, and affirmations that represent your goals and aspirations. By surrounding yourself with visual reminders of what you want to achieve, you reinforce your commitment to those goals every time you see your board. This tangible representation of your dreams serves to inspire you and keeps your motivation high, especially during difficult moments when you might feel like giving up.

Incorporating visualization into your daily routine can also amplify its effectiveness. Set aside a few minutes each day to practice visualizing your success. Whether it's in the morning to kickstart your day or at night to reflect on your achievements, consistency is key. As you make visualization a habit, you will find that it not only boosts your self-esteem but also helps you develop a positive mindset. This shift in perspective can make a significant difference in how you approach challenges and setbacks.

Finally, remember that visualization is just one part of the success equation. While it is essential to envision your goals, taking actionable steps towards them is equally important. Use your visualizations as motivation to prepare, practice, and persevere. When challenges arise, remind yourself of the images you have created in your mind. By combining visualization with determination and hard work, you will be better equipped to rise again after any setback, leading you on the path to achieving your dreams.

Planning for Life Beyond Challenges

Planning for life beyond challenges involves a proactive approach that empowers young adults to envision their futures despite setbacks. It is crucial to recognize that challenges are not the end of the road but rather opportunities for growth and self-discovery. As you navigate through your teenage years, setting clear goals and crafting a plan can help you move forward with confidence. This process begins with self-reflection to identify your passions, values, and aspirations. Understanding what truly matters to you lays the foundation for creating a meaningful life beyond obstacles.

Developing a roadmap for your future requires breaking down your long-term goals into manageable, actionable steps. Start by setting SMART goals: Specific, Measurable, Achievable, Relevant, and Time-bound. For instance, if you aspire to improve your grades, outline a study schedule that includes specific subjects and deadlines. This structured approach makes it easier to stay focused and track your progress. Regularly revisiting and adjusting these goals ensures that they remain relevant to your evolving interests and circumstances, allowing you to adapt and grow.

In addition to setting goals, building a support network is essential for thriving beyond challenges. Surround yourself with individuals who encourage and inspire you, whether they are friends, family members, or mentors. Engaging with a diverse group can provide different perspectives and resources that enhance your planning efforts. Don't hesitate to seek guidance or share your aspirations; collaboration often results in new ideas and solutions that you might not have considered alone. Having a reliable support system can also bolster your resilience as you face various obstacles.

Another vital aspect of planning for life beyond challenges is cultivating a positive mindset. Your thoughts and beliefs significantly influence your actions and outcomes. Practice self-compassion and remind yourself that setbacks are a natural part of life. Embrace a growth mindset by viewing challenges as opportunities to learn rather than insurmountable barriers. Techniques such as journaling, meditation, or engaging in hobbies you love can help maintain your mental well-being, making it easier to focus on your goals and aspirations.

Finally, embracing adaptability is key to successfully navigating life beyond challenges. The ability to pivot and adjust your plans in response to changing circumstances is a valuable skill. Life is unpredictable, and being open to new opportunities can lead you to unexpected paths that may align even more closely with your passions. Trust that the skills and resilience you develop while overcoming challenges will serve you well in the future. By being prepared and adaptable, you can rise again, transforming setbacks into stepping stones toward a fulfilling and successful life.

Embracing Change and New Opportunities

Embracing change can be one of the most daunting challenges young adults face, especially during a time of life filled with transitions. Change often brings uncertainty, which can create feelings of anxiety and fear. However, it is important to recognize that change is a natural part of life and can serve as a catalyst for personal growth and discovery. Understanding this can help you shift your perspective and view change as an opportunity rather than an obstacle.

When faced with change, it is essential to acknowledge your emotions. It is normal to feel overwhelmed, confused, or even resistant. Instead of suppressing these feelings, allow yourself to experience them. Journaling can be a helpful tool for processing your thoughts and emotions. Write down what you are feeling and why you think those feelings are arising. This practice not only provides clarity but also helps you identify patterns in your reactions to change, making it easier to navigate future transitions.

Once you have processed your emotions, consider the potential opportunities that change can bring. Every change, whether it's moving to a new school, starting a new hobby, or dealing with the loss of a friendship, presents a chance to learn something new about yourself and the world around you. Think about the skills you can develop or the new people you might meet. By reframing your mindset to focus on possibilities, you empower yourself to take proactive steps toward embracing change.

Moreover, surrounding yourself with supportive friends and mentors can make a significant difference in how you handle change. Engage in conversations with those who have experienced similar transitions. They can provide valuable insights and encouragement. Building a network of support not only offers reassurance but also fosters a sense of community. Knowing you are not alone can make the process of change feel less intimidating and more manageable.

Lastly, setting small, achievable goals can help you navigate the changes in your life. Whether it's dedicating time to a new interest or reaching out to someone new, these goals can help create a sense of direction and purpose during turbulent times. Celebrate each accomplishment, no matter how small, as it reinforces your ability to adapt and thrive. Embracing change is not just about enduring it; it's about recognizing the potential for growth and transformation that lies within every new opportunity.

www.ingramcontent.com/pod-product-compliance
Lightning Source LLC
LaVergne TN
LVHW010121170826
845678LV00012B/2526

* 9 7 9 8 2 3 0 9 2 1 7 9 0 *